THE ETYMOLOGY OF LORD RAM

A CULTURAL AND SCIENTIFIC OVERVIEW

DR. JAGADEESH PILLAI

Made with ❤ on the Notion Press Platform
www.notionpress.com

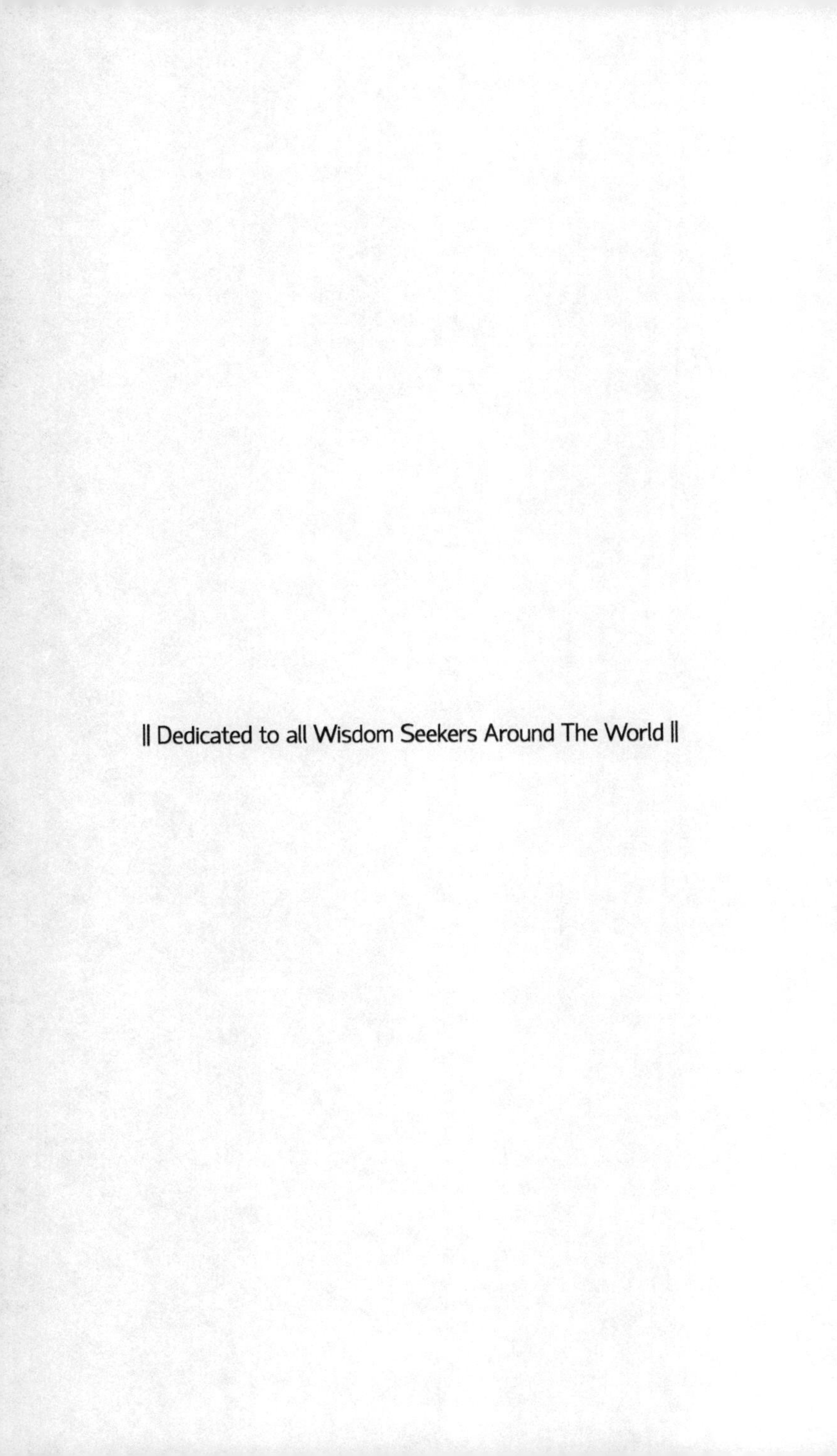

‖ Dedicated to all Wisdom Seekers Around The World ‖

Contents

Contents

Prayer

|| RAM RAM RAM ||

About The Author

Dr. Jagadeesh Pillai is a renowned Guinness World Record holder, writer, and researcher hailing from Varanasi, also known as the abode of Lord Shiva. With a Ph.D. in Vedic Science and a range of creative ideas and achievements, he is a true polymath. He is the author of more than 100 books including Research Publications. Although his roots can be traced back to Kerala, the people of Varanasi hold him in high regard and affectionately consider him one of their own.

Dr. Pillai has achieved four Guinness World Records in the following subjects:

1. "Script to Screen" - In this record, Dr. Pillai produced and directed an animation film within the shortest time possible, breaking the previous record set by Canadians. He has also received numerous national and international awards and recognitions for this achievement.

2. Longest Line of Postcards - For this record, Dr. Pillai created a line of 16,300 postcards on the occasion of the 163rd anniversary of Indian Postal Day. The event also included a questionnaire about the Indian flag.

3. Largest Poster Awareness Campaign - Dr. Pillai designed an awareness campaign on the subject of "Beti Bachao - Beti Padhao" (Save the Girl Child - Educate the Girl

Child) to achieve this record.

4. Largest Envelope - In tribute to the Indian Prime Minister's "Make in India" initiative, Dr. Pillai created a 4000 square meter envelope using waste paper to achieve this record.

5. Attempted - 70000 Candles on a 210 kg Cake - To celebrate the 70th Indian Independence Day, Dr. Pillai attempted to light 70,000 candles on a 210 kg cake, which was recorded in World Records India.

6. Attempted - Documentary on Dhamek Stupa of Sarnath in 17 Languages - Dr. Pillai attempted to create a documentary on the Dhamek Stupa of Sarnath, dubbing it in 17 different languages. The result of this attempt is currently awaiting confirmation from the Guinness World Records.

Dr. Pillai is skilled in teaching the Bhagavad Gita, a Hindu scripture, and is popular among young people. He has helped many young people improve their lives through his motivational teachings.

In addition to teaching, he has composed and sung

numerous Sanskrit Bhajans and patriotic songs.

He has also written and directed several short films and documentaries for awareness campaigns, and has volunteered with the police in both UP and Kerala to spread awareness about various issues through videos and photography.

He has a goal of writing thousands of books on Indian culture, Indian temples, and the lives of extraordinary people. Incredibly, he has produced and directed over 100 documentaries about the city of Varanasi, all on his own.

He has also helped and guided more than 25 boys and girls to achieve world records through creative and innovative methods. He is a multifaceted person who uses his intellect and the blessings given to him by God to excel in various areas. He is both a teacher and a student, always learning and teaching, and is able to master any subject he comes across.

He is a selfless social activist and motivational speaker who has overcome struggles and failures to become a successful and enthusiastic individual with a rich life experience.

In addition to his work with the Bhagavad Gita, he is also an efficient Tarot card reader, Astro-Vastu consultant, and a talented singer and composer. He has sung the entire Ram Charita Manas and Bhagavad Gita in his own compositions, and has sung the phrase "Lokah Samastha Sukhino Bhavantu" in 50 different languages. He is currently working on a detailed and scientific study of Vedas, Upanishads, Puranas, and the Bhagavad Gita. He has also composed and sung the Hanuman Chalisa and Gayatri Mantra in 108 and 1008 different compositions, respectively.

Awards - Four Times Guinness World Records, Winner of Mahatma Gandhi Vishwa Shanti Puraskar, Mahatma Gandhi Global Peace Ambassador, Kashi Ratna Award, Dr. APJ Abdul Kalam Motivational Person of the Year 2017, Mother Teresa Award, Indira Gandhi Priyadarshini Award, Bharat Vikas Ratna Award, Udyog Ratna Award, Vigyan Prasar Award, Poorvanchal Ratn Samman.

Preface

The Etymology of Lord Ram: A Cultural and Scientific Overview is a comprehensive examination of the origins, meanings, and significance of the name "Ram" in Hinduism and other Indian cultures. This book delves into the rich and complex history of the name "Ram," exploring its roots in ancient Sanskrit, the cultural and mythological contexts in which it is used, and its scientific and linguistic implications.

The name "Ram" is central to the Hindu tradition, as it is the name of one of the most revered deities in the religion. Lord Ram is revered as a symbol of righteousness, virtue, and leadership, and his story is told in the epic poem, the Ramayana. This book traces the evolution of the name "Ram" and its various meanings over time, highlighting its cultural and scientific significance.

The Etymology of Lord Ram is an invaluable resource for anyone interested in the history and meanings of this important name. It is a must-read for scholars of linguistics, mythology, religion, and South Asian studies, as well as for general readers interested in exploring the cultural and scientific dimensions of the name "Ram."

Prologue

I haven't yet transformed to that level to write on the subject of Lord "Ram", but I consider it my duty to share some of the influence of the land of civilization and culture on the earth in which I live. The way Maharishi Valmiki ji and Goswami Tulsidasji have described Lord "Rama", I am not even the dust of their feet. "Ram" is not just a name, but the name "Ram" or the word "Ram" is a mahamantra. Scholars say that the **"word" is Brahman**, so good things should be born in the mind and **divine words** come out of the mouth. God has given many more places in the body to remove dirty things. When the Divine Brahma's words comes out of the mouth, the mind will come pure and then more pure and divine speech will come out.

In this book, I have tried to write on the basis of my experiences about the greatness and miracle of the word "Rama" more than a God named "Ram.

Like everyone else, I have been hearing the names of many gods like Ram, Krishna, Shiva, Maa Durga since childhood. But just a few years ago, when some scholars of Kashi got the opportunity to know the science behind India's Vedic texts and history, such as Ramayana, Mahabharata, etc., they longed to learn more about all . Then one thing was understood that there is deep scientificity hidden behind every Vedic Sanskrit mantra from every letter of Sanskrit.

By chanting "Ram", a Chandal demon named Ratnakar transformed from a great Scholar like Valmiki and an epic like Ramayana was created. That's enough to understand what happens by chanting "Ram". Ratnakar was not asked by the Maharishis to chant the name of Lord "Shri Ram", just said to chant "Ram", "Ram" because the Maharishi already knew that the waves generated by chanting or hearing the word "Rama", "Ram" have the potential to destroy negative elements from our minds.

Of course, this work does not happen very quickly or in a day. By doing this day by day, many types of negative energy generated from many births or produced in this birth continue to destroy us and we continue to get inspiration to move forward in life with good compatibility and thinking. Therefore, this book is not only telling about worshiping a God named "Ram", but also to keep saying "Ram" "Ram" or trying to keep writing "Ram" "Ram" whenever you get a chance.

There are many methods of worshiping God and each method has its own science. But by chanting or writing the name "Ram" "Ram" we can achieve immense success in life. My eagerness to know and understand more and more about the greatness and scientificity of the name "Ram", I am presenting here whatever little knowledge I have gained during my efforts and search.

My only request is that even if someone is able to reduce the worship of God, but if someone understands the importance of the word "Ram", chant or write or listen to it, even this much can receive God's grace and be benefited in various ways.

CHAPTER ONE

Brief Introduction to 'Ram'

Lord Ram is a central figure in Hindu mythology and is revered as one of the most important deities in the Hindu pantheon. His story is told in a number of ancient Indian texts, including the Ramayana and the Ramcharitmanas, and he is revered as a symbol of righteousness, virtue, and courage.

In the Ramayana, Lord Ram is depicted as the prince of Ayodhya, a kingdom in ancient India. He is the son of King Dasharatha and Queen Kausalya, and is the eldest of four brothers. Despite his many virtues, Lord Ram faces a number of challenges and setbacks throughout his life, including a long exile from his kingdom and a difficult war against the demon king, Ravana.

Despite these challenges, Lord Ram remains steadfast in his commitment to dharma, or moral duty, and is able to overcome all obstacles through his strength, wisdom, and devotion. Through his actions and deeds, Lord Ram becomes a symbol of righteousness and virtue, and is revered as a great hero and role model in Hindu mythology.

CHAPTER TWO

The Mythological Origins of Lord RAM

Lord Ram, also known as Ramachandra, is a central figure in Hindu mythology and one of the most revered deities in the Hindu pantheon. According to Hindu belief, Lord Ram is the seventh avatar, or incarnation, of the god Vishnu and is revered as a symbol of righteousness, virtue, and courage.

The mythological origins of Lord Ram can be traced back to ancient Indian scriptures, such as the Ramayana and the Mahabharata. According to these texts, Lord Ram was born as the prince of Ayodhya, a kingdom in ancient India. He was the son of King Dasharatha and Queen Kausalya, and was the eldest of four brothers.

As a young prince, Lord Ram was known for his wisdom, strength, and noble character. He was a skilled archer and warrior, and was admired by all who knew him. Despite his many virtues, however, Lord Ram was not immune to the challenges and hardships of life. He faced numerous obstacles and setbacks throughout his life, including a long exile from his kingdom and a difficult war against the demon king, Ravana.

Despite these challenges, Lord Ram remained steadfast in his commitment to dharma, or moral duty, and was able to overcome all obstacles through his strength, wisdom, and devotion. Through his actions and deeds, Lord Ram became a symbol of righteousness and virtue, and is revered as a great hero and role model in Hindu mythology.

In addition to his mythological origins, Lord Ram is also an important historical figure in India. He is believed to have lived during the Treta Yuga, a period of great prosperity and cultural advancement in ancient India. His story and teachings continue to influence Hindu thought and practice to this day, and he is revered as a symbol of strength, virtue, and devotion.

Lord Ram is an important and revered figure in Hindu mythology and history. His story and teachings continue to inspire and guide Hindus around the world, and he is revered as a symbol of righteousness, virtue, and courage.

CHAPTER THREE

Importance of Invoking God

All human beings strive to live happily, but in modern times, many of us find ourselves feeling more stressed and less content. Fortunately, we can find solace in the power of prayer. The Upanishads tell us that in the Kaliyuga, the only way to overcome our problems is to chant the name of God.

In our busy lives, it can be difficult to find the time to practice karma, yoga, yagna, jnana, and other spiritual activities. Fortunately, we can still reap the same rewards by simply calling upon the name of God. Whether we call upon Him as Ram, Jesus, Nanak, Buddha, Krishna, or Rama, we can be sure that He will understand and provide us with the supreme welfare we seek.

No matter what language we use, God will always recognize our prayers. He does not require us to remember Him in any particular way or situation; all He asks is that we remember Him with love. When we call upon Him, He will provide us with the fruit of our meditation.

So, no matter what name we choose to call upon, we can be sure that God will answer our prayers and provide us with the peace and contentment we seek.

CHAPTER FOUR

The Science Behind The Word 'RAM'

The word "Ram" is a common name in Hinduism and has a number of meanings and associations. In Sanskrit, the word "Ram" is derived from the root "Raj," which means "to shine" or "to rule." As a result, the word "Ram" is often associated with ideas of leadership, strength, and radiance.

In Hinduism, the name "Ram" is often used as a shortened form of the name Ramachandra, which refers to the seventh avatar of the god Vishnu. As such, the name "Ram" is often associated with ideas of divine protection and guidance.

There are also a number of scientific theories and associations related to the word "Ram." In physics, for example, the term "ram pressure" refers to the force exerted on an object as it moves through a fluid or gas. This concept is often used in the study of celestial bodies, such as galaxies and stars, which can be affected by the pressure of the gases and particles that surround them.

In computer science, the term "random access memory"

(RAM) refers to a type of computer memory that can be accessed randomly, rather than in a predetermined order. This allows a computer to access and process data more quickly and efficiently.

The word "Ram" has a number of meanings and associations in Hinduism, science, and other fields. Whether used as a name, a scientific term, or a symbol, the word "Ram" carries a wealth of significance and significance.

Scienec and Effect of "Ram"

In this book, I am exploring the powerful effects of the word 'Ram' on our inner and outer worlds. Scholars say that *'Kalyug is only nama adhara, sumari sumari nar uttarhi para'* - that the power of the name is the only thing that can help us in this age. To understand how this works, I am sharing the effects of its use on many people.

When the word 'Ram' is said, a shape is formed on the air or sand, creating a special rhythm in the mind. Chanting 'Rama' continuously can expand the aura around our body. We all wish for physical happiness and wealth, but in the path of devotion, we don't need to offer money or objects to get God's blessings. All we need is a pure mind and dedication, and we can get everything from God, regardless of any other kind of power.

It is also important to understand how the word 'Ram' affects a person. Science tells us that we need evidence to believe the truth, but if we remember the Lord with a pure heart and dedication, God Himself will give us a thousand proofs. I have experienced the influence of people remembering the name 'Ram' without reasoning, as well as the lifestyle and influence of those who despised the name 'Ram' by reasoning and logic.

Therefore, it is important to set aside our arguments when we want to understand someone's influence. Scientists researching sound science say that the mind becomes calm when pronouncing the name 'Ram'.

The sound of a cuckoo brings us immense joy, and the name of Ram is associated with this feeling. The pronunciation of Ram is linked to the navel chakra of our body, which is shaped like a triangle (Δ). Its seed mantra is "Ram". This is one of the five elements and the source of the purest fire. This fire is capable of burning away all impurities without being contaminated itself. It is divided into three types: Surya, Jwala, and Jatharagni.

The power of Ram is connected to this same fire, and when we pronounce it, it has a transformative effect on our body and the aura around us.

CHAPTER SIX

Fire of "Ram"

Everyone knows the story of Maharishi Valmiki, who was once a dacoit, robbing and killing people. His name was Ratnakar, and he was a completely negative person, not even knowing how to pronounce the name **Ram**. But, as he began to chant **Ram-Ram**, he gradually started to pay attention and the name **Ram** had such a powerful influence on him that he became a great maharishi and composed the Ramayana.

This story serves as a reminder that if a demon-like robber can become a great scholar and maharishi by taking the name **Ram**, then we are in a much better position than a bandit today. The power of the name **Ram** can help us to overcome our negative thoughts and create positive ones that are simple and easy. By chanting the name **Ram**, we can unlock the knowledge and wisdom stored within us, just like heating ghee to spread its aroma. The waves of the name Ram can help any negative person to become positive, and this is the true power of **Ram**.

CHAPTER SEVEN

Etymology and Meaning of the Name "Ram"

Etymology and Meaning of the Name "**Ram**"

The word 'Ram' is derived from the sum of the suffix 'Dhan' in the '**Ram**' metal. 'Ram' metal means associated with doing ramne (residence, vihara). '**Ram**' is 'Raman' (meditative) in the heart of all beings, that is why he is also 'Ram'.

"Ramte kane kane iti ramah. "

CHAPTER EIGHT

Vishnu Sahasranama and "Ram"

If we consider the Vishnu Sahasranama, a result obtained by chanting the name of Shri Vishnu 1000 times, it is not feasible for everyone to remember all of the thousand names. However, it is much easier to chant the name of Ram three times. The last lines of the Vishnu Sahasranama, known as the Shri Ram Tarak Mantra, state: "Ram Rameti Rameti, Rame Rame Manorama Sahasranama Tattulyam, Ramnam Varane". This mantra is equivalent to chanting the entire Vishnu Sahasranama, and is also referred to as the Shriramrakshastotram. By chanting this mantra, one can receive the same result as chanting the thousand names of Vishnu.

CHAPTER NINE

"Ram" "Ram" and 108

There are many ways to worship God, one of which is chanting a mala of 108 grains while repeating a mantra 108 times. In today's busy world, it can be difficult to find the time to chant for so long. However, it is possible to achieve the same effect by simply repeating the name of Ram twice. This is because:

The Hindi alphabet consists of vowels and consonants, and the name Ram is made up of the 27th consonant, the 2nd vowel, and the 25th consonant. Therefore, chanting Ram once is equal to 54 times, and chanting it twice is equal to 108 times. This can be experienced firsthand, and is a great way to connect with the divine.

R + A + M = Ram

Now the 27th position of 'R'

Second place of 'A' vowel and

'M' comes in the twenty-fifth place.

therefore

(1) 27 + 25 = 54 ("Rama" once taken fifty-four times)

(2) 27 + 25 = 54 (five times by taking "Ram" a second time)

In total, it is equal to chanting the rosary 108 times. Its effect can also be seen by experience.

CHAPTER TEN

Addressing as "Ram Ram"

Those who rise early in the morning in the village and greet each other with a warm "Ram-Ram" do not need to separately worship Ram. There is a stark contrast between the tranquil lives of those who greet each other with Ram-Ram and those who simply say "Good Morning" in English. Those who address Ram with Ram appear to be more content, compassionate, loving, generous, and have more positive behaviors, while those who simply say "Good Morning" in English tend to be more exhausted, irritable, and self-centered.

Value of Gem as 'Ram'

When we sing or chant the name "Ram," both our mind and body are positively affected. Like a gold ornament that loses its luster, our bodies may lack a certain radiance. But if we adorn our bodies with the name "Ram," we become invaluable and precious.

Ravidas ji has also spoken about the power of the name "Ram" in many ways. Just as sandalwood infuses its scent into every molecule of water when placed in it, the name "Ram" similarly affects us on a deep level.

Another way to understand the importance of the name "Ram" is to think of a diamond, pearl, or any other precious gemstone. These items are always valuable to us, yet an empty thread holds little worth. However, if we weave a precious diamond into that thread, the thread becomes valuable and valuable.

Similarly, we are like a thread and if we weave the precious diamond of the name "Ram" into our bodies, we become invaluable. The name "Rama" brings with it the qualities of beauty, brightness, and purity, and anyone who disregards this diamond named "Ram" is foolish.

CHAPTER TWELVE

"Ram" and Charity

In the Kalyug, if we want to donate or give to Brahmins, we must become wealthy. However, in today's era, we see more poverty than wealth. Thinking of being poor or rich based solely on material resources would be misguided. It is easy to become materially wealthy in this age, but it is a blessing to be spiritually rich. To consider paper money as real wealth is to be ignorant. We need paper money to meet our needs, but it is also important to be spiritually wealthy. The most fortunate person is the one who chants the name of **Ram** every day and lives a life of joy and contentment. It is up to us to decide whether we want to become millionaires, billionaires, or even spiritual billionaires.

Chanting the name of Rama is a simple solution to living a happy life. Not only will it benefit the person you donate to, but it will also have a positive effect on you. Material money can buy many things, but it cannot buy peace of mind or joy. Chanting the name of Rama will bring you the pleasure and contentment you seek.

CHAPTER THIRTEEN

Sant Malook Ji Maharaj

Acharya Mukesh Bhardwaj ji from Shri Vrindavan Dham heard a beautiful account of the power of the name of Ram. It was said that even the most stubborn of people could be changed by the chanting of the name. Later, a great saint, Malook ji Maharaj, began to chant the name of Ram.

At a dharamshala in Ayodhya, at four o'clock in the morning, all the saints would start kirtan in the name of Mahatma Ram. There was a person in the same dharamshala who was disturbed by the kirtan and said to the Mahatma, "Do you people do Ram-Ram day and night? You have spoiled my sleep. What do you get by doing all this?" The Mahatma replied with great love, "We eat only the name of Ram. What we do, this whole world is eaten by them."

The man said in anger, "I earn and eat on my own. Do you keep saying anything?" Mahatma ji laughed again and said, "Believe it or not, Ram ji feeds everyone, including you. The person said, "I bet that I will chant the name of Ram only once today. I will see how your Ram feeds me. I won't eat anything for 24 hours. If Ram feeds me, I will become your disciple."

The man left his home, wondering if someone had forced him to eat something or if he had accidentally consumed it. He decided to go to the forest, where he found a huge tree laden with dense leaves. He climbed up the tree and thought that he would wait and see how Ram ji would provide for him.

Just then, some banjaras passed through the forest. It was almost evening and the sardar said, "Let's eat and drink." The smell of the hot food they cooked wafted up to the man in the tree, and he thought to himself, "There is merit in the Mahatma's words, the bread has come so far." But he decided to wait and see how Ram ji would provide for him.

The banjaras cooked more food than they needed, so they wouldn't have to cook again. Suddenly, the man heard the sound of bandits coming from the distance. The banjaras quickly left the food and ran away to save their lives. The bandits were hungry, but they were afraid that someone had deliberately added poison to the food because it was still hot. They debated amongst themselves, wondering if they should risk eating the food.

The hunger was so intense that all the robbers were desperate, and the man in the tree started trembling. The leaves shook, and the bandits saw him. Thinking he had poisoned the food, they were about to kill him. But the man quickly said, "Don't kill me, I'll come down!"

The bandits demanded that the man eat the food they had

provided, but he refused, citing his oath not to eat. He insisted that there was no poison in it, and that he could eat it without fear. The bandits grew increasingly suspicious of his refusal, and began to beat him. Despite his protests, they forced him to eat the bread.

The man thought to himself, "I have come to the forest to test the power of the name of Ram. I am eating this bread, but what glory is this? I am eating against my will." The next day, he wept at the feet of the Mahatma and begged for initiation. He declared that he did not want to return home, as he had nothing to eat or earn there. The Mahatma smiled and granted his wish, and the man was initiated into the Brij Mandal. He went on to become the most renowned saint of the region, Saint Shri Malukadas Ji Maharaj.

Maluka Dasji proclaimed, "The dragon and the bird may not be able to provide, but Rama is the ultimate provider of all."

CHAPTER FOURTEEN

"Ram" and Hanuman

The power of the name Ram is undeniable. Hanuman, is a testament to this fact. In The Ramayana, we see stones of all sizes floating in his name. Even the smallest of stones, upon which Setubandha was made by squirrels and apes, was buoyed by the glory of Ram. This name has the power to increase the movement of humans exponentially, as seen in the feats of Hanuman ji. Whether it was crossing the sea, taking a small form, or appearing in a huge form, Hanuman ji was able to accomplish his tasks by meditating on the name of Ram. We too can achieve success in our endeavors by chanting this name.

CHAPTER FIFTEEN

The glory of "Rama" by Ravana

Once, a saint related a beautiful incident that took place between the King of Lanka, Ravana, and his wife, Mandodari. According to the story, when Mandodari heard about the bridge being built to Lanka by the monkey army of Lord Rama, she went to Ravana and warned him to return Sita, Lord Rama's wife, to him or face dire consequences. She pointed out that the monkey army was able to build the bridge by throwing stones with the name of "Ram" written on them into the water and they were able to float on the water. If the name of "Ram" had such power, she asked, how powerful must the men who invoked it be?

Ravana, however, was dismissive of Mandodari's concerns and decided to prove to her the power of his own name. He took her to the beach and picked up a stone, on which he wrote his name "Ravana." He then closed his eyes and threw the stone into the sea. To Mandodari's surprise, the stone floated on the water.

Feeling confused and wanting to understand the truth, Mandodari asked Ravana how this was possible. Ravana explained that when he picked up the stone, he remembered the name of "Ram" and, after writing "Ravana" on it, swore to the stone that if the name of "Ram" had power, it would float, but if it did not, it would sink. The stone floated because of the power of "Ram," not because of his own name.

Additionally, another episode is known by Ravan, in which during the war between Rama and Ravana, Ravana recognizes that Ram is not an ordinary human. He is the embodiment of three gods; Brahma, Vishnu, and Mahesh. He explains that when Rama draws his bow, it seems as if there is a four-faced Brahma looking from all four directions. When Rama releases the arrow, it appears as if there are a thousand faces of Vishnu. And when Rama attacks, he becomes as destructive as Rudra. He said that Rama possesses the powers of all these three gods.

CHAPTER SIXTEEN

Power of the word "Ram"

According to the story, it is believed that if a person has been invoking the name of "Ram" since childhood, then that person cannot be killed intentionally. It is said that the influences and qualities that a mother has seen and heard during her pregnancy are imparted to the child in the womb. The person who has been fed the potion or "ghutti" named "Ram" will never die an untimely death.

In the story, Hanuman, who is a great devotee of Lord Rama, is said to have been given the name "Ram" as a potion or ghutti at the time of his birth, and that is why he was able to evade death. The story states that when Guru Vasishtha visited Lord Rama's court, Hanuman was so absorbed in his devotion to Lord Rama that he did not notice the arrival of the Guru. This made Guru Vasishtha very angry and he demanded that Hanuman be punished for this slight. Lord Rama, instead of being sad, accepted his Guru's words and announced the death penalty for Hanuman on the banks of the Saryu river.

When Hanuman went to take orders from his mother,

Anjani, she told him that since his birth she had been chanting the mantra "Ram" and had fed him the same potion "Ram" from that time, thus no one could kill him, only he needs to chant the name "Ram" continuously. Hanuman then, taking the blessings of his mother, went to the banks of the Saryu river and started chanting the name "Ram" continuously. Lord Rama reached the bank of the river and shot his immortal arrow many times, but it couldn't harm Hanuman. Surprised, Guru Vasishtha asked Lord Rama why his arrow was not affecting Hanuman. Lord Rama explained to him that the name "Ram" is much bigger than his name and Guru Vasishtha, understood and left the royal court, went to a cottage and started chanting the "Ram" mantra continuously.

CHAPTER SEVENTEEN

Inner Management of Ram

If you look at the life of Shri Rama, it is filled with a series of unfortunate events. From being born a prince, to being exiled to the forest for 14 years, to his wife Sita being kidnapped, to crossing the ocean and burning Lanka, to Sita giving birth to two sons without Rama's knowledge, to Sita sacrificing her life in the forest - it is clear that Rama's life was far from successful. But why do we still worship him? It is because no matter what happened, Rama never lost his composure. He never renounced the principles and values of his life, and he always maintained his balance and inner peace.

We bow our heads to this quality, for it is the essence of inner management. Rama is a symbol of peace and joy, no matter how much trouble is thrown his way. He is an example of how to remain balanced and happy in the face of adversity.

CHAPTER EIGHTEEN

"Rama" a balanced, stable pattern

Sadhguru, a spiritual teacher and founder of Isha Yoga, has explained the significance of the name "Rama" and how it can be an icon for us to follow. According to Sadhguru, when we constantly immerse ourselves in "Rama," we begin to develop the same qualities as Lord Rama. He explains that when we are living a normal life, we tend to focus on the shortcomings of people around us, but when we are influenced by the name "Rama," we start paying more attention to the positive aspects of people, just like how we can name a tree by the fruit it bears.

Sadhguru further explains that for creating great civilizations in the world, it is important to have the right qualities, and Lord Rama is an icon all over the world, who for six thousand years, has inspired generations to walk on the path of truth, respect, love, compassion, and purity. He is considered as a replica who never takes any step in haste, rather he is a statue of stability. He is a model of someone who always takes decisive steps in a balanced manner and with consciousness.

Sadhguru highlights that when Lord Rama resides within us, we become free from anger and that Lord Rama was such a great man that even after killing the ten-headed demon king, Ravana, who had kidnapped his wife Sita, he still regretted it as one of the ten heads of Ravana had good thoughts and was a great devotee of Shiva, a devout religionist and a great scholar. If we are blessed with the qualities of Lord Rama in our lives, Sadhguru says, our life will change completely and this will change the way we work, think, and behave.

CHAPTER NINETEEN

"Ram" and Cells in the Body

Chanting the name "Ram" is believed to bring a sense of peace and solve problems in one's life. It is said that the chant of this name attracts the attention of Lord Hanuman, who is known to be a great devotee of Lord Rama. Chanting the name "Ram" is said to create vibrations that are felt by the 50 trillion cells in our body, equivalent to 1.4 volts. This, in turn, has a positive effect on our behavior and thinking.

When we are around positive people, it is believed that we tend to adopt their positive qualities and want to spend more time with them. Similarly, when we chant the name "Ram" repeatedly, it is said to bring positive changes in us and make us more like Hanuman - someone who is known for his devotion, selflessness, and the ability to accomplish difficult tasks. It is also believed that by chanting "Ram-Ram" and connecting with Hanuman, we can overcome difficult situations and destroy our ego, making us more humble and compassionate.

Kali–Santaranopanishad

The Kali-Santaranopanishad provide an effective way to navigate the side effects of this era. The Upanishads believe that the veil of ignorance is not easily lifted, and the mantras contained within them can help to destroy this veil. Once the veil is destroyed, the Brahman or the form of the Self is revealed to the sadhaka in the same way that the sun is revealed when the clouds dissipate.

When Narada asked Brahma for the best mantra to achieve this, Brahma replied that the mantra containing 16 letters is as follows:

**"Hare Ram Hare Ram, Ram Ram Hare Hare Hare
Hare Krishna Hare Krishna, Krishna Krishna Hare Hare"**

This mantra is said to be the most effective remedy found in all four Vedas, and its constant chanting can free one from all kinds of unity, Salokya, Samya, Saarya, Saarak, Sakadiya, etc. It is said that if one chants this mantra three crore times, they will be liberated from the sins of Brahman, murder, theft, and the sins of gods and humans.

All sins of the entire half are purified at once, and one can achieve Moksha at the earliest opportunity. Moksha at the earliest opportunity, and this is the Upanishad.

CHAPTER TWENTY-ONE

Rama purnatapinyupanishad

The Ramapurnatapinyupanishad is connected to the ancient Upanishadic tradition. It consists of five volumes, each referred to as an Upanishad. In this section, it is said that Rama is the one who brings about the death of the Rakshasa due to his sinful acts. He is known as Ram in human form. The infinite, eternal bliss, the Supreme Soul, and the Supreme Being are known as Parabrahma Parameswara in the Bitiyopanishad of this volume. It is said that, just as the great banyan tree is present in the small seed, the entire universe is present in the form of the seed of Ram Rupa. The three idols of Brahma, Vishnu, and Mahesh are located on the Rama and The Car, and the three types of powers of creation, preservation, and destruction (Raudri, Jyeshtha, and Vama, arising from the nad and the seed) are also situated in the same Ram.

This Upanishad mentions that The Ram in human form, and is said to be the embodiment of the infinite, eternal bliss, the Supreme Soul, and the Supreme Being. The Upanishad states that, just as the great banyan tree is present in the small seed, the entire universe is present in the form of the seed of Ram Rupa. Furthermore, the three idols of Brahma, Vishnu, and Mahesh are located on the Rama and The Car, and the three types of powers of creation, preservation, and destruction (Raudri, Jyeshtha, and Vama, arising from the nad and the seed) are also situated in the same "Ram".

CHAPTER TWENTY-TWO

Sree ramottartapiyupanishad

The Ramottarpinyupanishad is an Upanishad that includes a dialogue between the sage Yajnavalkya and Bharadwaj. In it, Yajnavalkya explains the significance of the name "Ram" and the effects of chanting it.

According to Yajnavalkya, the first letter of the Shadakshara Mantra "Ram Raamaya Namah:" (which is the first letter "Ra" of "Ram") is an expression of his own personal experience. He says that the name "Ram" is a cue from the 10 generations of his previous life and the next 10 generations, and that it has the power to destroy all sins, including sins of anger, greed, vision, theft, and murder.

CHAPTER TWENTY-THREE

Taraka Mantra

Yajnavalkya also mentions the **Tarak Mantra**, which is a six-character Brahma Saudalakshara Mantra, formed by the combination of the letters "Night + Ra + Ma + Ma + y + Ma + M:." He explains that this mantra has the power to create sound, shake, and emotion, and that it is a powerful mantra for achieving the same fruits as sacrifices. He further states that chanting the name "Ram" is as productive as giving gold in charity.

Yajnavalkya also tells the story of Lord Shankar (Lord Shiva), who prayed to Lord Rama by chanting the mantra "Shriram" and pleased Lord Rama, who granted him a boon. Lord Shiva asked for the release of his body of life at the Manikarnika Tirtha in Kashi or on the banks of the Ganges. Lord Rama also granted him the boon to preach the sermon in the right ear of any dying person.

CHAPTER TWENTY-FOUR

Ram Ramapati Bank

This year marks the 91st anniversary of the Ram Ramapathi Bank, a unique financial institution located in Kashi, India. Unlike traditional banks, this bank does not deal in rupees, but rather in loans of the name of Ram. Here, more than 19 billion Ram is written by devotees of all religions, including Hinduism, Islam, and Christianity.

The Ram Ramapathi Bank offers loans to people from India and abroad, free of charge. All that is required is a paper and a wooden pen with red ink. Devotees believe that their problems are solved by taking a loan from this bank. The bank is open from 8 AM to 8 PM every day, and its address is available for anyone who needs a spiritual loan.

Address ; Kashi Vishwanath in the lane. 5/35Tripura Bhairavi Road, Dashashwamedh, Varanasi Uttar Pradesh-221001

CHAPTER TWENTY-FIVE

Lord Ram and Five Elements

In Hinduism, the Five Elements, or Pancha Tatwa, are believed to be the fundamental building blocks of the universe. These elements are Earth, Water, Fire, Air, and Space, and they are believed to be present in all living and non-living things.

Lord Ram, one of the most revered deities in Hinduism, is believed to be connected to the Five Elements in a number of ways. According to Hindu belief, Lord Ram is the seventh avatar, or incarnation, of the god Vishnu, who is associated with the element of Space. This connection suggests that Lord Ram embodies the infinite and the absolute, and is a symbol of the divine presence in the universe.

In addition to his association with the element of Space, Lord Ram is also believed to be connected to the other elements in various ways. For example, his association with righteousness and virtue is often linked to the element of Earth, which represents stability and solidity. His courage and strength are sometimes associated with the element of

Fire, which represents passion and energy. And his wisdom and understanding are often linked to the element of Air, which represents intellect and clarity.

In Hinduism, Lord Ram is also believed to be connected to the element of Water in a number of ways. One way in which this connection is often depicted is through the story of Lord Ram's exile, during which he is said to have crossed the river Sarayu on his way to the forest. This crossing is often seen as a metaphor for Lord Ram's ability to navigate and overcome challenges and obstacles in life.

The element of Water is also associated with emotions and the human mind, and Lord Ram is sometimes depicted as having a deep understanding and empathy for the feelings and needs of others. This aspect of his character is often linked to the element of Water, which represents the qualities of the human mind and emotions.

In addition to these associations, Lord Ram is also sometimes depicted as a protector and guardian of the natural world, and the element of Water is often seen as an important aspect of this role. In Hindu mythology, Lord Ram is sometimes referred to as "Varuna," after the god of the ocean, and is believed to have the power to control and protect the waters of the world.

The connection between Lord Ram and the element of Water is an important aspect of Hindu belief and symbolism. Through this connection, Lord Ram is seen as a symbol of wisdom, understanding, and the ability to navigate and overcome challenges in life.

CHAPTER TWENTY-SIX

'RAM' in Hindu Festivals and Rituals

Lord Ram is an important deity in Hinduism and is revered as a symbol of righteousness, virtue, and leadership. He is also seen as an embodiment of dharma, the principle of moral order that upholds the universe. As such, Lord Ram is an important figure in many Hindu festivals and rituals.

One of the most important Hindu festivals that centers around Lord Ram is Ram Navami, which celebrates his birth. This festival is typically celebrated in the month of March or April, depending on the Hindu calendar. On this day, devotees visit temples, offer prayers, and perform devotional songs and dances in honor of Lord Ram.

Lord Ram is also an important figure in other Hindu festivals such as Navaratri and Diwali. Navaratri, which means "nine nights" in Sanskrit, is a festival that celebrates the divine feminine, with one of the nine nights dedicated to worshipping Lord Ram. During the festival of Diwali, devotees light lamps and perform prayers to honor Lord Ram's return to Ayodhya after defeating the demon king, Ravana.

In addition to festivals, Lord Ram is also an important figure in Hindu rituals and ceremonies. For example, his name is often invoked in wedding ceremonies and other rituals as a way to seek blessings and guidance. Lord Ram is also depicted in many Hindu temples, where devotees offer prayers and make offerings to him.

Lord Ram is an important figure in Hinduism and is revered for his righteousness, virtue, and leadership. His significance is reflected in the many festivals and rituals that center around him.

CHAPTER TWENTY-SEVEN

RAM and HANUMAN

The story of the Ramayana, one of the two major Sanskrit epics of ancient India, centers around the life of Rama, an avatar of the god Vishnu. Rama is portrayed as the ideal man and king, and the epic tells the story of his journey to rescue his wife, Sita, from the demon king of Lanka, Ravana. Hanuman, the divine monkey-like being, plays a crucial role in the epic as a devoted servant of Rama. The mental connection between Rama and Hanuman is a deeply spiritual one, as Hanuman's unwavering devotion to Rama serves as a model for the ultimate surrender of the ego to a higher power.

Throughout the Ramayana, Hanuman demonstrates his unwavering devotion to Rama in a number of ways. He is always ready to serve Rama and do his bidding, no matter what the task may be. When Rama and his brother, Lakshmana, are banished from their kingdom and forced to live in the forest, Hanuman becomes one of their loyal companions, protecting them from harm and helping them in their quest to rescue Sita.

Hanuman's devotion to Rama is also evident in the way he willingly puts himself in danger to serve Rama's cause.

When Rama and Lakshmana are captured by the demoness Surpanakha, Hanuman fights to rescue them, even though he knows he is no match for the powerful demoness. Similarly, when Rama asks Hanuman to go to Lanka to find Sita and assess her condition, Hanuman does not hesitate, even though he knows that the journey will be fraught with danger.

Hanuman's visit to Lanka is a key turning point in the Ramayana, as it sets the stage for the final showdown between Rama and Ravana. When Hanuman arrives in Lanka, he is confronted by the demon king's army of rakshasas. Despite being vastly outnumbered, Hanuman is able to defeat them through his superior strength and agility, as well as his divine powers.

Once he has made his way into Lanka, Hanuman meets Sita and learns of her plight. Sita has been held captive by Ravana, who hopes to use her as leverage to force Rama to abandon his quest to rescue her. Hanuman is deeply moved by Sita's plight and vows to do everything in his power to help her.

In order to fulfill his promise to Sita, Hanuman must first find a way to get back to Rama with the news of her whereabouts. To do this, he sets fire to Lanka, knowing that the flames will attract Rama's attention. When Rama and his army finally arrive in Lanka, Hanuman is there to greet them and guide them to the place where Sita is being held.

The mental connection between Rama and Hanuman is evident throughout the Ramayana, as Hanuman's unwavering devotion to Rama is a constant theme.

Hanuman's faith in Rama inspires him to undertake incredible feats of strength and courage, and his selfless service is a model for all those who seek to surrender their ego to a higher power. Ultimately, it is this mental connection that enables Hanuman to play a pivotal role in the story of the Ramayana, helping Rama to rescue Sita and defeat the demon king of Lanka.

Other Books Of The Author

1. The Moments When I Met God
2. Kashiyile Theertha Pathangal
3. GURU GYAN VANI
4. Abhiprerak Gita
5. ASSI SE JAIN GHAT TAK
6. Hopelessness of Arjuna
7. The Soul and It's True Nature
8. Sense of Action (Karma)
9. Action through Wisdom
10. Action through Wisdom
11. THEORY AND PRACTICAL OF EVERY ACTION
12. LOGICAL UNDERSTANDING OF THE SUPREME
13. THE IMPERISHABLE SUPREME
14. Yatra Nishadraj se Hanuman Ghat Tak
15. Yatra Karnatak Ghat se Raja Ghat Tak
16. Yatra Pandey Ghat se Prayagraj Ghat Tak
17. Yatra Ranjendra Prasad Ghat se Dattatreya Ghat Tak
18. YaatraSindhiya Ghat se Gwaliar Ghat Tak
19. Yatra Mangala Gauri Ghat se Hanuman Gadhi Ghat Tak
20. Yatra Gaay Ghat Se Nishad Ghat Tak
21. MAA GANGA, GHATEN EVM UTSAV
22. Ganga Arti Dev Deepavali evam Any Utsav
23. Potentials of Digitalized India
24. VEDIC CONSCIOUSNESS
25. A Brief Introduction to Vedic Science
26. Kashi ke Barah Jyotirling
27. IMPACT OF MOTIVATION
28. Let's have a Milky Way Journey
29. Color Therapy in a Nutshell

30. Rigveda in a Nutshell
31. Yajurveda in a Nutshell
32. Samveda in a Nutshell
33. Atharva Veda in a Nutshell
34. Ayushman Bhava - Ayurveda
35. Srimad Bhagavad Gita and Upanishad Connection
36. Srimad Bhagavad Gita - an attempt to summarize each chapter.
37. Facts and Impact of Nakshatra
38. Astro Gems - NAVARATNA
39. Ekadashi - A Concise Overview
40. A Concise View of Hanuman Chalisa
41. Inspirational Gita
42. Nakshatraranyam
43. Summary of 18 Mahapuranas
44. Synopsis of 18 Upa Puranas
45. Rigvediya Upanishads
46. Shukla Yajurvediya Upanishads
47. Krishna Yajurvediya Upanishads
48. Samavediya Upanishads
49. Atharvavediya Upanishads
50. The Seven Great Sages
51. From Rocket Scientist to President Dr. APJ Abdul Kalam
52. The Visionary's Voice - Quotes of Dr. APJ Abdul Kalam
53. The Wisdom of Swami Vivekananda: Insights and Inspiration from a Legendary Spiritual Teacher
54. Ayurvedic Remedies from the Garden
55. Sages and Seers
56. Rising Strong – Motivational Stories of Women
57. Beyond Flames -Mystery stories of Funeral Ghat Manikarnika
58. The Origins of Tulsi: A Look at the Mythological Roots of the Plant"

Contact

DR. JAGADEESH PILLAI

PhD in Vedic Science

Four Times Guinness World Record Holder

Winner of Mahatma Gandhi Vishwa Shanti Puraskar and
Global Peace Ambassador

Gemology, Astro & Vastu Consultant - Spiritual Counselor

Consultant for designing World Record Ideas

Efficient Tarot Card Reader

9839093003

myrichindia@gmail.com

drjagadeeshpillai@facebook

drjagadeeshpillai@instagram

jagadeeshpillai@youtube

www. JAGADEESHPILLAI.com

|| RAM RAM RAM ||

• 53 •

|| LOKAHA SAMASTHAHA SUKHINO BHAVANTU ||